Dear Grandma,

I am writing to you to wish you a happy New Year.

I don't like Paris very much and am looking forward to returning to your place again soon. The holidays started a few days ago, and I have tried to work hard, like you told me to, but my whole body is covered with spots. I spend a lot of time scratching them.

Please tell Aunt Emily my canary Lulu is very cute and sings beautifully. I am very happy to teach her. To make her happy, I bought her a beautiful new cage with my own allowance.

Goodbye, Grandma. Here's a big hug. Do you feel it? Also, happy New Year to Uncle Charles, Aunt Emily, and Uncle Anton. You'll see me again soon.

Your loving grandson,

Henri

Mason Crest Publishers, Inc.
370 Reed Road
Broomall, Pennsylvania 19008
866-MCP-BOOK (toll free)

Illustrations copyright
© 2001 Yan Thomas
Published in association with
Grimm Press Ltd., Taiwan
Printed in Taiwan.

1 3 5 7 9 8 6 4 2

Library of Congress Cataloging-in-
Publication Data:

on file at the Library of Congress.

ISBN 1-59084-155-7
ISBN 1-59084-133-6 (series)

Great Names
TOULOUSE-LAUTREC

My name is Comtesse Adele de Toulouse-Lautrec. In my time, it was common for relatives to marry in order to preserve the purity of their aristocratic blood. Thus, I married my cousin, Comte Alphonse de Toulouse-Lautrec.

We lived in Albi, France, and on November 24, 1864, I gave birth to our first child, Henri. We all adored him, especially his grandmothers. Everyone who saw him loved him. He was a happy child, as chirpy and active as a cricket. When he wasn't around, our home was dull and quiet. He brought as much life into our lives as 20 people.

His father was a keen horseman, hunter, and painter, and Henri soon showed similar enthusiasms. As a small child, he loved to paint crows. Then, at his cousin's christening, when he was only four years old, he noisily insisted on signing the register as the adults were doing. Of course, he didn't know how to sign his name, so instead he drew a crow. This made everyone laugh.

To us, Henri was the most precious gift imaginable. When he was eight, we moved to Paris so we could give him a better education.

Although he didn't let us down and was always in the top five students, we knew Henri really preferred painting. If I wasn't around to supervise, he would draw in his textbooks and exercise books. When I scolded him, he would reply, "All these letters and punctuation marks are so boring! It would be more fun to be a horse eating grass."

Actually, I was often fascinated by the things he drew. When he wasn't around, I would look at them. Sometimes, I would burst out laughing, especially at the images of his teachers and classmates.

Henri's younger brother died in 1868 before he was two years old. Henri was all I had left. We let him do what he wanted most of the time, even when he was willful and naughty. Since he was a sickly child, we didn't have the heart to scold him.

We realized that Henry was much shorter than other boys his age. (Henri grew to be about five feet tall [154 cm.]) His legs gave him lots of trouble. They were either covered in spots or painful. The doctor was afraid he had some incurable, rare disease. The worst of it was that bad luck just kept coming. I'll never forget May 31, 1878, when our bouncy, young 13-year-old boy fell off a chair and broke his left thigh. A year later, he and I were walking in the woods when he fell again and broke his right leg. These two major accidents meant he had no chance of growing taller, and his legs gradually withered also.

Dear Uncle Charlie:

Although I am not well, I have something very exciting to tell you. The more I draw, the better I get. I am very happy with myself. You are, of course, the first person I want to hear my good news because it is your support and encouragement that has made it possible for me to progress in my sketching. I think you will be happy for me. Although Mama is still not very happy about my wish to give up studying, I knew I would eventually be able to persuade her and make her realize how determined I am to be an artist.

How I wish I had a teacher who could teach me color and brushwork!

Your Future Artist and
Loving Nephew,
Henri

Dear Grandma,

I can't run around much these days and life seems very dull. At least my hands aren't the problem; otherwise even lying in bed I wouldn't be able to paint! Mama has brought me home. I am to have electric therapy. Uncle Charles had this and got better. My right foot is better now, but my left leg is still lame. I hope the doctor is right and this is just my first response to the treatment. I am a bit better, really. Please don't worry about me.

Your loving grandson,
Henri

Poor Henri didn't want to worry us and was always putting on a bright face. He faced all his difficulties with optimism and humor.

One day when several friends came to visit, he made an announcement in front of everybody. "My dear family, don't cry over my misfortunes. I'm so clumsy, that it's not worth worrying about. I have you and many good friends, which makes me very fortunate. You are all too good to me. I'm spoiled."

I couldn't wait for him to finish. Tears welled up in my eyes and I rushed from the room. This was what he was like. If your heart ached for him, he would try to set it at ease.

Because moving around was difficult for Henri, he had to give up his outdoor interests such as hunting and riding. Gradually, his time was divided between art, music, reading, and, of course, painting. He often spent the whole day painting. He sometimes wrote stories that he illustrated in watercolors. His Uncle Charles never stopped encouraging him and never stopped hoping he would find something that would make him happy.

At first I worried that being an artist was too hard a life for Henri. After seeing how determined he was, I let myself be slowly persuaded. When he graduated from high school, I said he could go to Paris and study at the Princeteau Painting Studio.

He returned to Paris in 1881 to take the high school graduation examinations but failed. He tried again the next year and was successful.

The teachers at Princeteau made Henri feel very welcomed. They admired his work. Soon, they recommended that Henri find more technically proficient teachers, so he began to study with Leon Bonnar, Cormon, and other respected teachers. During this time, he was full of energy. Henri would leave early most days for the studio to paint. Then he would go out with his fellow students to paint outdoors and to have fun.

Henri and his friends spent most of their time visiting the home of Rene Grenier and his wife. They regularly organized masked balls, plays and other entertainment. Henri showed me some photos of him wearing many different costumes. They looked like a lot of big children playing. Henri appeared to be as innocent and eager as he had when he was a child. Sometimes he played a Japanese samurai, sometimes a troubadour, sometimes a woman, and sometimes a striking Spanish dancer.

After seeing those photos, I felt much happier. It was obvious his friends would not reject him or mistreat him because of his appearance. On the contrary, he got along with everyone well.

One day I met one of his friends who said to me, "Madame Adele, I am proud for you because you have an intelligent, smart, funny, and generous-spirited son. He is our soul. Without him, something would be missing." Hearing these words reminded of Henri when he was our four-year-old cricket, our family's fount of happiness.

Until he was 20 years old, Henri lived with me. Later, I decided to return to the country, to Malrome, to live. I couldn't get used to living in Paris, and Henri had his own life to live. It was time for us to part. It was hard for me to leave him, but I knew he had to make his own way no matter how it turned out.

In the summer of 1884, Henri didn't come home for the holidays. I knew he was deeply involved in his work. He made time to write to me and tell me about his life so I wouldn't worry.

1884

Dear Mama,

I can't resist shouting! Long live Manet! Long live the revolution! Impressionism has blown into our studio! I'm so happy. Cormon's old brain needs a good cleaning out. The Impressionists have brought painting alive. I yearn to be like them. I want to slowly get rid of the dark palette I've learned and let light splash onto my canvas. I want to go outdoors and paint much more.

Cormon has invited me to help him do the illustrations for

Victor Hugo's collected works. You will certainly feel proud of your son.
I am the only student in the class to be invited and this will be the first
money I have earned in my career as a painter.

Your homesick, lonely son,

Henri

The son of aristocrats, Henri had always been treasured and protected.
We taught him traditional etiquette, gave him as much knowledge as
possible so he could become an educated gentleman.

Although he chose to be an artist, we still hoped he would become
a respected teacher at the academy or paint portraits of the court. But he
never listened to us. He spent all his time in bars and places like that. He
didn't take the academy entrance exams. His father was very angry.

1884

Dear Mama,

I have moved to Montmartre with some friends. I don't want to hide this from you because you are the person I respect most in this world, but I hope you will understand.

Montmartre is a very lively place. There are coffee bars, bars, dance halls, and concert halls everywhere. The streets are busy and the sounds of singing and dancing go on till the moon is high in the night sky. I love it here, not because I want pleasure, but because the people, whether singer, dancer, craftsman, or prostitute, are all full of life. They are not like the gentlemen and ladies of this world concerned about etiquette and form. They live life as it is. Most important of all, no one here cares about an ugly, short-legged, big-armed, potato-nosed man.

I can enjoy life fully here, as any normal person does.

Your loving son,

Henri

1885

Dear Mama,

　　Please forgive me for taking so long to reply to your letter, but please believe that every day I have been almost desperate to tell you my good news myself.

　　I have met a very talented singer, Aristide Bruant, in Montmartre. He is tall and broad, honest and open. We are like old friends already. Most important, he has hung my paintings in his dance hall and has asked me to paint posters for his new songs. Now everyone is talking

about my posters, and Burant is famous. If you heard him, you would laugh.

Your dear son has fallen in love with a woman called Suzanne Valadon. She is a model introduced to me by Edgar Degas.

Summer is nearly here. I will come and pay my respects to you and visit everyone back there. At this moment, all I can think of is swimming in the river, or going fishing.

1889

Dear Mama,

    For some time I have been very sad because Suzanne and I have split up. Once I discovered she was manipulating my feelings and was only interested in money, I came to my senses and decided there was no point in loving someone like her. The sound of laughter flows in from outside; there's no need for me to sigh here alone.

    For France, 1889 is a good year. Parisians are wildly celebrating. Everyone is heading for the Eiffel Tower. Even Montmartre feels different. The opening of the Moulin Rouge has brought new life and energy to the district, attracting all of Paris. My work, *At the Cirque Fernando,* is hanging in the main hall.

    A lot of people I know come here to experience the creative spirit. One of the famous people at Moulin Rouge, Louise Weber, who is called by her nickname La Goulue, has created a dance that has all the night owls in Paris captivated. My brush is also in love with her. I can't resist drawing her.

1881

Dear Mama,

Painting posters is endless pleasure. It is hard to describe the sense of achievement I have when I return to the studio with my sketches to think and organize. First I look at them as the viewers do to see if they attract me or not. Then I look at them as an artist seeking the best way to create.

Moulin Rouge has asked me to create publicity posters for them to win back some of their customers. Jane Avril, Yvette Guibert, and others of whom you have heard me speak, all feature on my posters, which are all over Paris. Moulin Rouge is popular again, and its owner is extremely grateful to me. Its stars are equally grateful. Other cabarets are fighting for my services but, as you know, I don't just paint for anyone!

Jane Avril is a lovely woman. She appreciates art and literature more than any other singer I've met. She can dance passionately, relax with my guests, or sit quietly and watch me paint, admiring my work from the bottom of her heart. Even in Paris there is no one else like her! Please keep it in mind that I am not a common painter. Only people of talent and flair win my approval!

Another piece of good news is that the work I exhibited in the salon exhibition this year was very well received. One critic said, "The way he paints faces and captures personalities allows you to feel their spirit and tragedies."

The times are changing and the critics are moving with them. I am participating in many future invitation exhibitions, so I must not slacken. Give all the women a hug for me. I love everyone.

1892

Dear Mama,

You are a good woman and are bound to be pleased and excited at the wonderful luck that is soon to be mine. A friend mentioned my name to the greatest singer of the era, Yvette Guibert. Today, in her dressing room, she politely asked me to paint her. This is a dream come true! Many famous artists have painted her. I want to do something different. The family won't be able to feel my joy, but you are different. I know you will understand.

Another artist and I are designing an album for her. It will be a limited edition of 100 copies. I am sure that with her fame and my talent,

it will cause a sensation. I never imagined what would come from painting a few posters. Now they are calling me "The Creator of the Modern Poster."

There are even some canny collectors competing to get some of my earlier works. I have heard that one of my posters sells for near 20 francs. Heavens! Can you believe it?

I have to thank Maurice Joyant for this success. He has given me lots of good advice and has constantly encouraged me to have an exhibition. Next year I have agreed to let him organize a solo exhibition of my work. Quite frankly, I'm still a bit nervous about it. Goodbye for now, Mama.

Your son,
Henri

For quite a long time I worried that my little Henri would be blinded by the showy life of Montmartre. For these last few years, he has been as excited as a small child. He told me everything. I can't judge his actions and behavior by the standards used for other people, because I am all too conscious of the pain he bears, far more than ordinary people will ever know! I can feel the demand for progress he makes on himself. In every letter he reports every small success with such excitement that I know that his painting is far more important to him than anything else in the world.

I know that I must understand my child. Moreover, I must believe in him and support him. I know his friends, Maurice Joyant and others, are all very good people.

1895

Dear Mother-of-the-Artist,

Since my successful solo exhibition organized by Maurice, I have a flood of invitations to participate in exhibitions. Nearly every day there are negotiations, framing, printing, transporting pictures, attending openings, or so it seems. Please tell Father that, if he looks down on Montmartre, he should at least believe the *Revue Blanche*. Its chief editor invited me to join their meetings, at which France's finest writers and artists gather. I am so happy and honored to produce a poster for him.

Henri

Success brings pressure and can cause people to lose their way. Henri started drinking heavily. His friends, such as Maurice, his doctor, and his family tried to persuade him to stop. Sometimes things were better, sometimes they were worse. It was as though there was a curse on him that wouldn't go away and brought him trouble time after time. In March 1899, I was forced to send him to a mental hospital for treatment.

1899

Dear Maurice,

My savior and benefactor, you know me well and know I am not sick. I'm simply subject to delusions and am forgetful. Thank you for your letter. We have to work together to let everyone know I'm fine. Please send me a few printmaking tools and inks, a box of deep brown watercolor, some brushes, a wax pen for marking the stone, some good black ink, and some good paper. I will prove I haven't lost my mind. I am completely healthy!

Henri

Maurice suggested that Henri do a painting of the circus to prove he was sane and well. Henri did just that, producing 40 pictures all from memory. All of them were so brilliant that everyone was surprised. The doctors were forced to admit they had misdiagnosed his problem. Two months later he was released.

However, I am afraid Henri is not able to resist the temptation of alcohol, so I arranged for a relative, Paul Viaud, to come and look after him and prevent him from drinking.

For a time, Paul and his cousin accompanied Henri and helped him escape the shadow of alcoholism. As Henri's health was poor, they took him out in boats or carriages as often as possible or went to the races and other such outdoor activities.

In 1890, he fell in love with the opera *Messaline* and painted several paintings on that theme. I was very pleased. He was living a healthy life and producing some new pieces on new themes.

Just when I was feeling so proud of my son, I found out he was drinking secretly behind our backs. He even poured wine into the cavity inside his walking stick! As soon as I found out, I had him brought back home to Malrome to recover. But it was too late. He grew thinner and thinner. He couldn't bend his legs, and he was suffering from disease. He was so sick, that he was unable to eat. The doctors could do nothing.

September 8, 1901 was a very long day. Henri's father and I waited anxiously throughout the night. Henri's closed eyes and weak breathing was all the reward we got. During the early hours of September 9, Henri died in my arms. He was only 37.

Henri's father insisted on driving the hearse himself at the funeral. He said, "I want my son to travel to his final resting place as a gentleman." With a crack of the whip over the horses, he drove Henri on his final journey in this life.

July 30, 1922

Dearest Boy,

    After struggling for many years, Gabriel has finally succeeded in opening a gallery to honor you. The Minister of Education and Arts gave a very moving speech at the grand opening. I am sure you heard everyone's praise of you up there in heaven.

    My child, I have missed you so these 11 years, and even though I'm now a gray-haired woman, I still hear you singing and see your smiling face. Last night I dreamed you came and took me back to the house we lived in 40 years ago. Everyone was standing around our lively, energetic cricket who was standing and singing. When I woke up, the room still rang with the laughter and song. Suddenly I saw a bright fire warming everyone and bringing light into the lonely darkness. I suddenly understood. You burned your life in exchange for the freedom of creating art and eternal glory.

    I will be proud of you forever.

Mama

Adele

BIOGRAPHY

Author Diane Cook is a journalist and freelance writer. She has written hundreds
of newspaper articles and writes regularly for national magazines, trade publications,
and web sites. She lives in Dover, Delaware, with her husband and three children.